# WHEN A FELLER NEEDS A FRIEND

## AND

### OTHER FAVORITE CARTOONS

by

*Briggs*

( Clare Briggs )

DOVER PUBLICATIONS, INC., NEW YORK

Published in Canada by General Publishing Company, Ltd., 30 Lesmill Road, Don Mills, Toronto, Ontario.
Published in the United Kingdom by Constable and Company, Ltd., 10 Orange Street, London WC 2.


*When a Feller Needs a Friend and Other Favorite Cartoons by Clare Briggs,* first published by Dover Publications, Inc., in 1975, is a new selection from the seven-volume set *The Selected Drawings of Clare Briggs; Memorial Edition,* published by Wm. H. Wise & Co., New York, in 1930.


*International Standard Book Number: 0-486-23148-8*
*Library of Congress Catalog Card Number: 74-22556*

Manufactured in the United States of America
Dover Publications, Inc.
180 Varick Street
New York, N.Y. 10014

# PUBLISHER'S NOTE

Clare A. Briggs was one of the outstanding newspaper cartoonists of the early twentieth century. His specialty was the kindly depiction of the everyday pleasures and pains of the lower middle class, in big cities or in small towns. He was particularly successful in evoking—and preserving for us—the feelings and activities of boys growing up in late nineteenth-century America. Though he created some notable strips, he is best remembered for a variety of series, generally with some catchy motto as title or refrain: "When a Feller Needs a Friend," "Ain't it a Grand and Glorious Feelin'?" "Somebody's Always Taking the Joy Out of Life" and numerous others. His syndicated drawings were eagerly awaited by millions, and his characters suggested radio shows and films.

Briggs was born in Reedsburg, Wisconsin, on August 5, 1875. His family moved to Lincoln, Nebraska, when he was fourteen. He attended the University of Nebraska from 1894 to 1896 and studied draftsmanship as well. In 1896 he went to St. Louis, getting a job on the Globe-Democrat there in that year, and on the Chronicle in 1898. His next move was to New York, where he worked on Pulitzer's World during 1898 and 1899. Up to this point, he was primarily a reportorial sketch artist rather than a cartoonist.

Beginning in 1900, Briggs became a part of William Randolph Hearst's fast-growing empire. Hearst had bought the New York Journal in 1895. Newspaper cartoons and comic strips were already phenomenally popular and of real consequence to a paper's circulation. By 1896 Hearst had enticed the great cartoonist Richard F. Outcault (creator of The Yellow Kid and, later, Buster Brown) away from the World, initiating

CLARE BRIGGS

a sensational battle for comic artists that would last for many years. In 1900 Hearst acquired Briggs—as a cartoonist —but did not keep him in New York. Instead Briggs was sent to Chicago to inject vitality into the American, Hearst's latest venture. In 1902 the Examiner joined Hearst's Chicago holdings, and Briggs drew for that paper, as well as the American, until 1907. Then he was on the Chicago Tribune until 1914.

In 1914 Briggs returned to New York permanently, joining the staff of the Tribune (later Herald-Tribune), where he remained until his death at the age of 54 on January 3, 1930. All the material in this volume dates from his Tribune days; it has been selected (on the basis of draftsmanship, humor, imagination and variety) from a seven-volume memorial collection of Briggs' work published in the year of his death. Repre-

sented are the three motto series mentioned above, the newspaper series "The Days of Real Sport," "That Guiltiest Feeling," "There's at Least One in Every Office," "Real Folks at Home," "Wonder What . . . Thinks About," "How to Start the Day Wrong," "Movie of a Man," "It Happens in the Best Regulated Families," "Tedious Pastimes," "Handy Man Around the House," "Kelly Pool" and "Old Songs," and selections from the books Golf and Oh Man. The very popular family situation strip "Mr. and Mrs." was not included in the memorial collection, presumably because it was still being run (it was continued for some years by Arthur Folwell).

Briggs' draftsmanship, always firmly controlled and observant, varies from rather careful work, in which tradition and training are apparent, to clever quick sketches. The single most important influence on his production was the work of the distinguished cartoonist John T. McCutcheon (Pulitzer Prize, 1931), Briggs' senior by five years and a Chicago colleague. McCutcheon had preceded Briggs both in depictions of small-town boys and in the use of motto series. On the other hand, Briggs' influence on later artists is incalculable. Even the most rapid sampling of the present volume will show to what an extent it is still operative today.

"DESERTED"

THE TRAGEDY OF BELONGING
TO THE KIND OF PEOPLE WHO WILL
TAKE A FELLER WAY OUT IN SOME
LONELY SPOT — AND LOSE HIM·····

6    WHEN A FELLER NEEDS A FRIEND

8   WHEN A FELLER NEEDS A FRIEND

12    WHEN A FELLER NEEDS A FRIEND

WHEN A FELLER NEEDS A FRIEND 13

14    WHEN A FELLER NEEDS A FRIEND

WHEN A FELLER NEEDS A FRIEND   17

20   WHEN A FELLER NEEDS A FRIEND

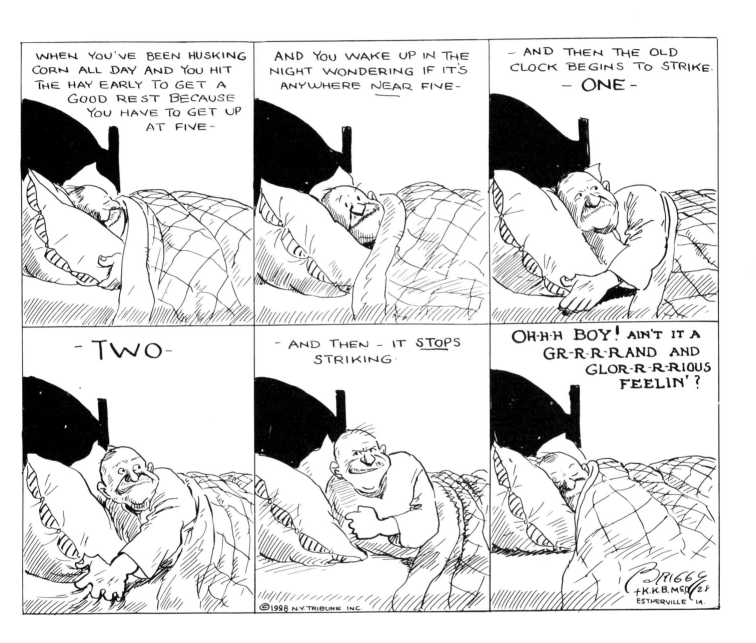

YOU AND YOUR SWEETIE HAVE A FALLING OUT— AND FOR A WHILE THE BOTTOM SEEMS TO HAVE DROPPED OUT OF YOUR WORLD—

YOU CAN'T EAT— YOU CAN'T SLEEP ——— AND YOU **HATE** EVERYBODY

YOU THEN DECIDE TO GO IN FOR SOULFUL THINGS——— TAKE UP MUSIC AGAIN——— WRITE POEMS OF PASSION OR A GREAT NOVEL

THEN YOU DECIDE YOU DON'T CARE A D——N ANYWAY ... AND YOU'RE GOING IN FOR DANCING AND PARTIES AND HAVE A GENERAL GOOD TIME

HUH

SNAP

AND YOU MEET A **NEW** MAN WHO FALLS FOR YOU AND MAKES LOVE **DIVINELY**— AND HE'S **TWICE** AS FASCINATING AS THE OLD LOVE

KATHERINE— I'M MAD OVER YOU—— I **MUST** AND **SHALL** HAVE YOU !

—AND YOU DECIDE YOU'RE JUST A FICKLE TRIFLING WOMAN—— BUT !-!!— OH-H-BOY !! AIN'T IT A **GR-R-R-RAND** AND **GLOR-R-R-RIOUS** FEELIN'!?

Briggs +K.

24   AIN'T IT A GRAND AND GLORIOUS FEELIN'?

WHEN YOU ARE LEAVING THE RESTAURANT YOU DISCOVER A **TEN DOLLAR BILL** IS MISSING. YOU KNOW YOU HAD IT THE NIGHT BEFORE AND **YOU KNOW** YOU HAVEN'T SPENT IT

- YOU WERE SAVING IT TO BUY A **BIRTHDAY** GIFT FOR YOUR SWEETIE! AND YOU MOAN AND WHIMPER AS YOU TRUDGE HOME THROUGH THE RAIN.

- AND YOU TRY TO BELIEVE YOU LEFT IT IN THE BOOKSTORE YOU WERE IN - BUT WHO EVER RETURNS MONEY FOUND -? NOBODY!

- AND NEXT MORNING YOUR FELLOW WORKERS ASSURE YOU PESSIMISTICALLY THERE ISN'T A CHANCE IN THE WORLD OF YOUR GETTING IT BACK! CAN'T ANYBODY SAY A CHEERFUL WORD? NOBODY!

- BUT YOU DECIDE TO CALL UP THE BOOKSTORE ANYWAY — YOU MAY AS WELL DO _THAT_

- AND THE BOOK-KEEPER SAYS "YES WE FOUND IT CALL THIS EVENING"- OH-H-H- BOY! AIN'T IT A GR-R-R-RAND AND GLOR-R-RIOUS FEELIN'?

TA-A- TUTTY TA TYA -

AIN'T IT A GRAND AND GLORIOUS FEELIN'?

SOMEBODY'S ALWAYS TAKING THE JOY OUT OF LIFE

SOMEBODY'S ALWAYS TAKING THE JOY OUT OF LIFE

HECTORIN'
THE GIRLS

THE HECKLERS

LONG
PANTS

- THE GIANT CRACKER -

©1928 N.Y. TRIBUNE INC.

JUST AS YOU ARE
ABOUT TO LIFT THE OLD
GATE - YOU SEE THE OWNER
BACK OF A TREE -
## JUST IN TIME —

THERE'S AT LEAST ONE IN EVERY OFFICE

## The Street Sweeper

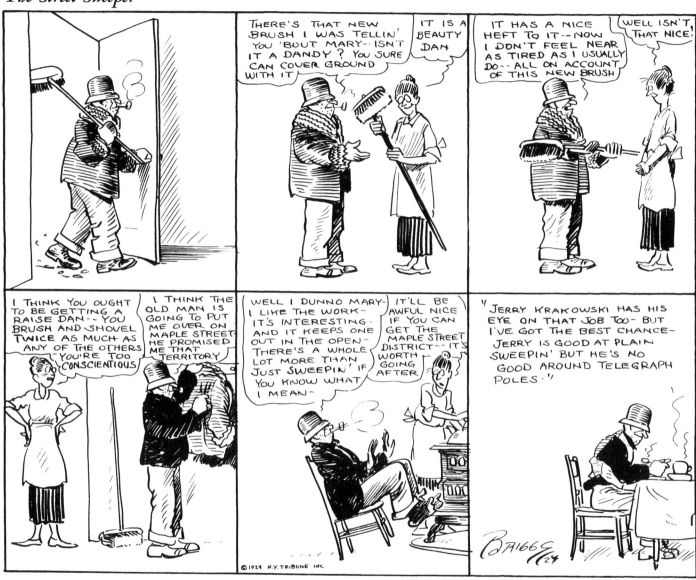

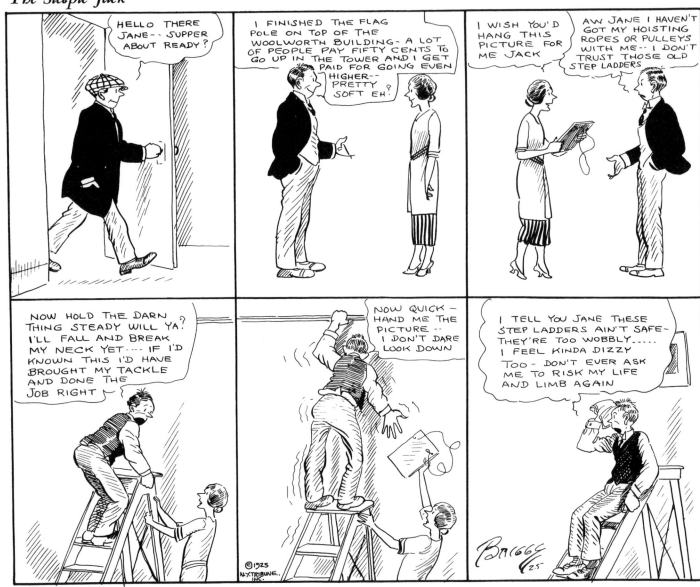

## A Traffic Cop

## The Hod Carrier

## The Song Writer

## The Orchestra Leader

## The Street Astronomer

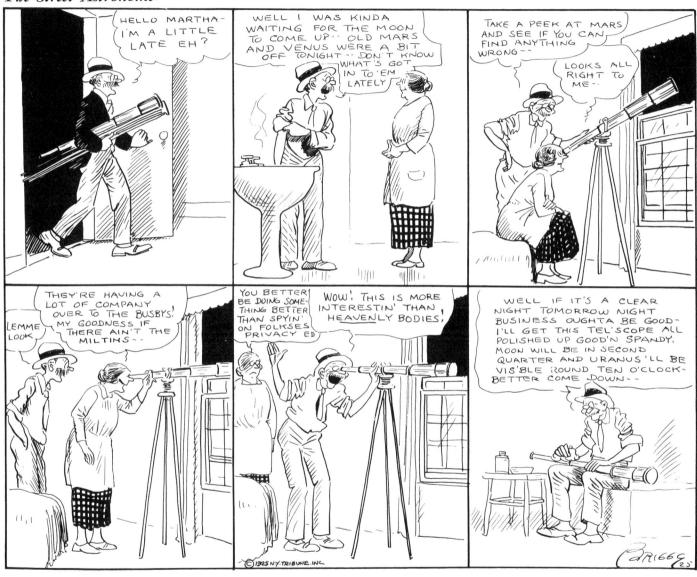

# *The Writer of Slogans*

## The Writer of Mystery Tales

## The Soda Clerk

## The Department Store Santa Claus

## The Ocean Hopper

## The Radio Announcer

## Wonder What a Kettle Drummer Thinks About Between Taps

I'VE A LITTLE HEADACHE THIS EVENING -- I CAN'T ACCOUNT FOR IT .... MUST BE SOMETHING I ATE - ONE OF THE SECOND VIOLINS IS A BIT OFF-- I'LL BET IT'S THAT BIG STIFF GIOVANNI -

I HATE THIS PIECE-- IT DOESN'T GIVE ME VERY MUCH OF A CHANCE -- STILL - THE NEXT NUMBER IS WHERE I SHINE ... I HOPE THAT BUNCH OF BRASSES WILL BE A LITTLE MORE PIANISSIMO TONIGHT -

WELL I SUPPOSE I MAY AS WELL GET READY FOR MY LAST NOTE ... IT'S A VERY IMPORTANT NOTE TOO--IT BRINGS OUT THE REST OF THE PARTS BUT THOSE BOOBS PROBABLY DON'T APPRECIATE IT -

THAT HEADACHE - I JUST CAN'T ACCOUNT FOR IT --A FEW GRAINS OF ASPERIN WOULDN'T DO ME ANY HARM- THIS DRUM HAS BEEN A LITTLE OFF LATELY --- AT THAT IT'S A BIG HELP TO THIS BUNCH OF FATHEADS IF I DO SAY IT MYSELF -

HERE'S WHERE I COME IN- I HOPE THAT CONDUCTOR WILL GIVE ME A LITTLE ATTENTION. -- AN AUDIENCE LOVES A GOOD KETTLE DRUM -

- AH-H- PERFECT! I GUESS THAT MAKES 'EM SIT UP AND TAKE NOTICE-

## *Wonder What a Girl in the Chorus Thinks About*

WELL HERE GOES THE SECOND ENCORE OF THIS ROTTEN NUMBER - GEE-E-E WHIZ

I GET SO SICK OF THIS NUMBER - BUH-LIEVE ME I COULD DO BETTER OR I'D CRAWL OFF'N DIE

THAT'S A CUTE LOOKIN' KID IN FRONT - I GOT HIS EYE A COUPLA TIMES, I S'POSE HE'S GOT A IDEA I'M SMILIN' AT HIM THE POOR FISH

I HOPE THIS IS THE LAST TIME - I'M SO TIRED I COULD FLOP ON A PICKET FENCE AND ENJOY A GOOD REST-

OH FOR TH' LUVA MIKE! ANOTHER ENCORE! I DON'T SEE WHAT THEY IS IN THIS PUNK SONG - I'M NEARLY DEAD-

- IF I COULD GET A JOB IN ANOTHER SHOW I'D JUMP THIS ONE 'N THAT'S NO CRACKED ICE DREAM EITHER -- I'D LIKE TO LIGHT ON A LIVE ONE ONCE BEFORE I CROAK

THAT WAS SOME PARTY LAST NIGHT! - I AIN'T GOT NO BUSINESS GOIN' OUT LIKE THAT - THERE'S THAT SIMP GIVIN' ME THE EYE AGAIN-

MAYBE HE WANTS TO FRAME UP A DATE - HE LOOKS LIKE HE'S ONLY A KID - YOU NEVER CAN TELL THO' - I'LL ASK CAMILLE WHAT SHE'S GOT ON FOR TONIGHT - I'D LIKE TO GO OUT AND MAKE A NOISY PARTY - I'LL GIVE HIM A SMILE 'N KID 'IM ALONG'

## *Wonder What a Public Drinking Fountain Thinks About*

I'M HAVING AN AWFUL BUSY SUMMER. I'M SO POPULAR···· IT DIDN'T USED TO BE LIKE THIS

I SURE DO MEET A FUNNY BUNCH OF PEOPLE···· LAMP THIS ONE FOR INSTANCE··· IT'S A GOOD THING I'M NOT TICKLISH·

THIS GUY HAS AN AWFUL THIRST—WHY THE POOR THING IS PARCHED···· HE MAKES A SIPPING NOISE LIKE A HORSE—THE FISH!

I WISH PEOPLE LIKE THIS WOULDN'T GET SO CLOSE···· THIS BIRD MUST HAVE HAD A BIG NIGHT

NOW—
HERE'S THE KIND OF FOLKS I LOVE TO SERVE··· THIS KID IS ONE OF MY MOST APPRECIATIVE PATRONS ··· HE SIMPLY WALLOWS IN ME—

THIS TYPE COMES AT ME WITH A DO OR DIE EXPRESSION···· A FACE LIKE A DRIED LEMON···· I'LL BE GLAD WHEN SHE'S THROUGH—

HERE'S ANOTHER HANG OVER···· OTTO IS A HARD WORKING GUY AND TO HIM I'M ONLY A FIRE EX—TINGUISHER··· THATS RIGHT GET IT ALL OVER YOUR FACE—

WELL IT'S ABOUT TIME SOMETHING LIKE THIS CAME ALONG···· I THINK I'M ENTITLED TO SOME REWARD———

## Wonder What a Dog with a Fancy Knit Blanket on Thinks About

WHAT DO YOU THINK OF A WOMAN THAT'LL GO TO WORK AND WISH A THING LIKE THIS ON ME? ON **ME**— YES **ME**

! WAS **NEVER** MORE MORTIFIED IN MY LIFE— WHAT IF MY LADY FRIEND SHOULD SEE ME IN THIS MAKE-UP— SHE'D THINK ME A SISSY

GEE— I THINK I HEAR JIMMY COMING— I DON'T WANT HIM TO SEE ME— I KNOW HE'LL DES-**PISE** ME AND NEVER TAKE ME ALONG WITH 'IM ANY MORE

I USED TO BE HAPPY AND GAY— NOW LOOK AT ME— HAVE A LOOK—

I COULD BAWL MY EYES OUT— WHAT DID I EVER DO TO DESERVE THIS DISGRACE OW-OO~OO~O~

WOW~OO~OO WHAT WILL MY PALS THINK— THEY WON'T WANT TO BE SEEN WITH ME **EVER** EVER~EVER~

I KNOW WHAT I'LL DO— I'LL HIDE MYSELF—— GO INTO SECLUSION AND NEVER BE SEEN AGAIN~

OH THE PITY OF IT— THE DISGRACE—

BRIGGS 19

## *Wonder What a Babe in Arms Thinks About*

MY POP IS TAKING ME **SOME PLACE** ON THE STREET CAR AND IT'S TERRIBLE ...... AND THE CAR IS CROWDED — AND POP HAS TO HANG ON TO A STRAP

GEE IT MAKES ME SEASICK -- WHY DOESN'T HE STAND STILL--HE SWAYS BACK AND FORTH AND SIDEWAYS LIKE EVER'THING

MY FATHER SWEARS PRETTY MUCH, GUESS HE'S KINDA SORE ON ACCOUNT OF HAVIN' TO HOLD ME -- HE'S HAVIN' AN AWFUL SERIOUS TIME

WHOA. WE ALMOST TURNED OVER THAT TIME ····· IT'S QUITE A ROUGH TRIP I'LL TELL THE WORLD

POP IS MAD 'CAUSE THE CAR STOPS SO MUCH — NOW WE'RE GOING AROUND A CURVE AND POP IS GRUNTING AND MUTTERING TERRIBLE- I CAN HEAR HIM PLAINLY·

© 1917 N.Y. TRIBUNE INC

HE TELLS ME TO HOLD ON TIGHT - EVERY.BODY FOR THEMSELVES FROM NOW ON

I'VE GOT A STRANGLE HOLD ON DAD BELIEVE **ME!** I GUESS HE'S CHOKIN' 'CAUSE I HEAR A QUEER RATTLE IN HIS THROAT

HERE WE ARE OFF THE STREET CAR AND DAD AND I ARE GLAD OF IT.. HE SAYS "NEVER AGAIN" BUT HE SAID THAT BEFORE — HE'S A GOOD NATURED MAN MY POP IS

Briggs '27

# *Wonder What a Microphone Thinks About*

THIS IS ONLY A SAMPLE OF THE THINGS I HAVE TO PUT UP WITH. THIS BIRD IS SINGING HE THINKS - I NEVER HEARD WORSE - HE'S HAD GARLIC - PHOOY-

HERE'S A LITTLE LADY SINGING SOME-THING ABOUT A LITTLE GARDEN FAIR - SHE'S FUNNY TO LOOK AT-

A BASSO PROFUNDO AND HE'S A LONG - WINDED BABY- WHAT A BORE - IT'S THINGS LIKE THIS THAT MAKES ONE DESPONDENT

SHE'S TELLING FOLKS ABOUT GOOD THINGS TO EAT AND SHE LOOKS HALF STARVED - I'LL BET IF SHE SAW HALF THE THINGS SHE TALKS ABOUT, SHE'D BURST RIGHT OUT INTO TEARS

HERE'S A GUY WHO IS TELLING AN EAGER AUDIENCE ALL ABOUT AFFAIRS OF THE WORLD AND THE SOLUTION OF ALL OUR ILLS.... I'LL BET THERE'S AN AWFUL HUSTLE OF DIAL TURNING IN RADIO HOMES RIGHT NOW

HONEST- NO FOOLING- SHE'S TELLING FAIR WOMEN THE USE OF BEAUTY CREAMS - TEE - HEE -

©1929 N.Y TRIBUNE INC.

THIS KINDLY OLD CORMORANT IS GIVING THE KIDDIES A BED TIME STORY. IT'S JUST AS WELL THEY CAN'T SEE HIM OR THEY'D LIE AWAKE ALL NIGHT

WHAT A HEADACHE! WHAT A LIFE! WHAT TH -

BRIGGS 29

# Wonder What An Actress in the Love Scene Thinks About

## Wonder What Circus Acrobats Talk About

## Wonder What a Muskallunge Thinks About

## *Wonder What the Wife of a Movie Hero Thinks About*

TAKE A LOOK AT THAT PHOTOGRAPH OF MY HUSBAND! YOU'D THINK HE WAS A CLOSE RELATION TO A SAINT-- HE'S A HOT SKETCH

HERE HE IS AS BEAUREGARD LEE, THE DASHING YOUNG HERO IN A ROMANCE OF THE SOUTH- OH-H-H

PIFFLE!

A COWBOY MAKE-UP! MY STARS! I THINK IF HE SAW A COW HE'D RUN FOR HIS LIFE-- TWO GUN PETE! GEE WHIZ! IF A GUN WENT OFF BEHIND HIS BACK HE'D FAINT AWAY

HERE'S A LOVE LETTER FROM A GIRL THAT SAYS "YOU ARE MY IDEAL, MY HERO"-- SHE OUGHT TAKE A LOOK AT HIM SOME MORNING REAL EARLY- HE DOESN'T LOOK LIKE ANYBODY'S HERO I'LL TELL THE WORLD

HERE'S A GIRL WHO WRITES "YOU ARE ADORABLE, MY SOUL-MATE"...... SHE CAN HAVE IT-- WITHOUT A STRUGGLE

HERE'S ANOTHER ONE SAYS "HOW LUCKY IS THE WOMAN WHO IS YOUR WIFE, CONSTANTLY BY YOUR SIDE, HAPPY WITH YOUR CARESSES" THAT'S A HOT ONE! IF SHE ONLY KNEW WHAT I THINK OF HIS "CARESSES"

© 1926 N.Y. TRIBUNE, IN C.

HONESTLY CAN YOU BEAT IT-- SHE CALLS HIM THE HANDSOMEST MAN IN THE WORLD-- WELL HE ISN'T SO BAD AT THAT-

HERE'S AN INTERVIEW THAT QUOTES HIM AS SAYING HIS HOBBY IS HIS LITTLE WIFE AND HOME! HE HASN'T BEEN HOME FOR SIX MONTHS

BRIGGS '26

## Wonder What a Mosquito Thinks About

## *Wonder What a Christmas Gift for Friend Wife Thinks About*

HE HAS PUT ME ON THE TOP CLOSET SHELF BUT ONLY TEMPORARILY.... HE IS TERRIBLY AFRAID I'LL BE DISCOVERED BY HIS WIFE BEFORE CHRISTMAS

NOW I'M IN A TRUNK IN THE ATTIC --- HE STILL FEELS UNEASY... THINKS SHE MIGHT START RUMMAGING AROUND

SO HE NEXT PUTS ME UNDER THE DRESSER - BUT IT'S TOO EXPOSED

NOW I'M BACK OF A NICE WARM RADIATOR BUT UNLESS HE TURNS OFF THE HEAT IT ISN'T GOING TO BE SO COMFORTABLE -

I'M A CONSTANT WORRY TO HIM... HE SAYS HE'LL BE GLAD WHEN CHRISTMAS IS OVER SO I'LL BE OFF HIS MIND --- HERE I AM UNDER HIS BED -

WELL WHERE NEXT!? BACK OF HIS OWN PORTRAIT... IF SHE TAKES A NOTION TO THROW THIS CHROMO AWAY, WHICH SEEMS QUITE REASONABLE, I'M DISCOVERED SURE -

AH - I THOUGHT SO! CHUCKED DOWN IN THE BOTTOM OF THE CANE AND UMBRELLA RACK. THE MAN'S NEARLY CRAZY TRYING TO FIND A PLACE HE THINKS SAFE -

HERE I AM BACK IN TOWN IN HIS OFFICE DESK.... I'LL BET HE GOES HOME CHRISTMAS EVE AND FORGETS ME

## *Wonder What a Chicken Crossing the Road Thinks About*

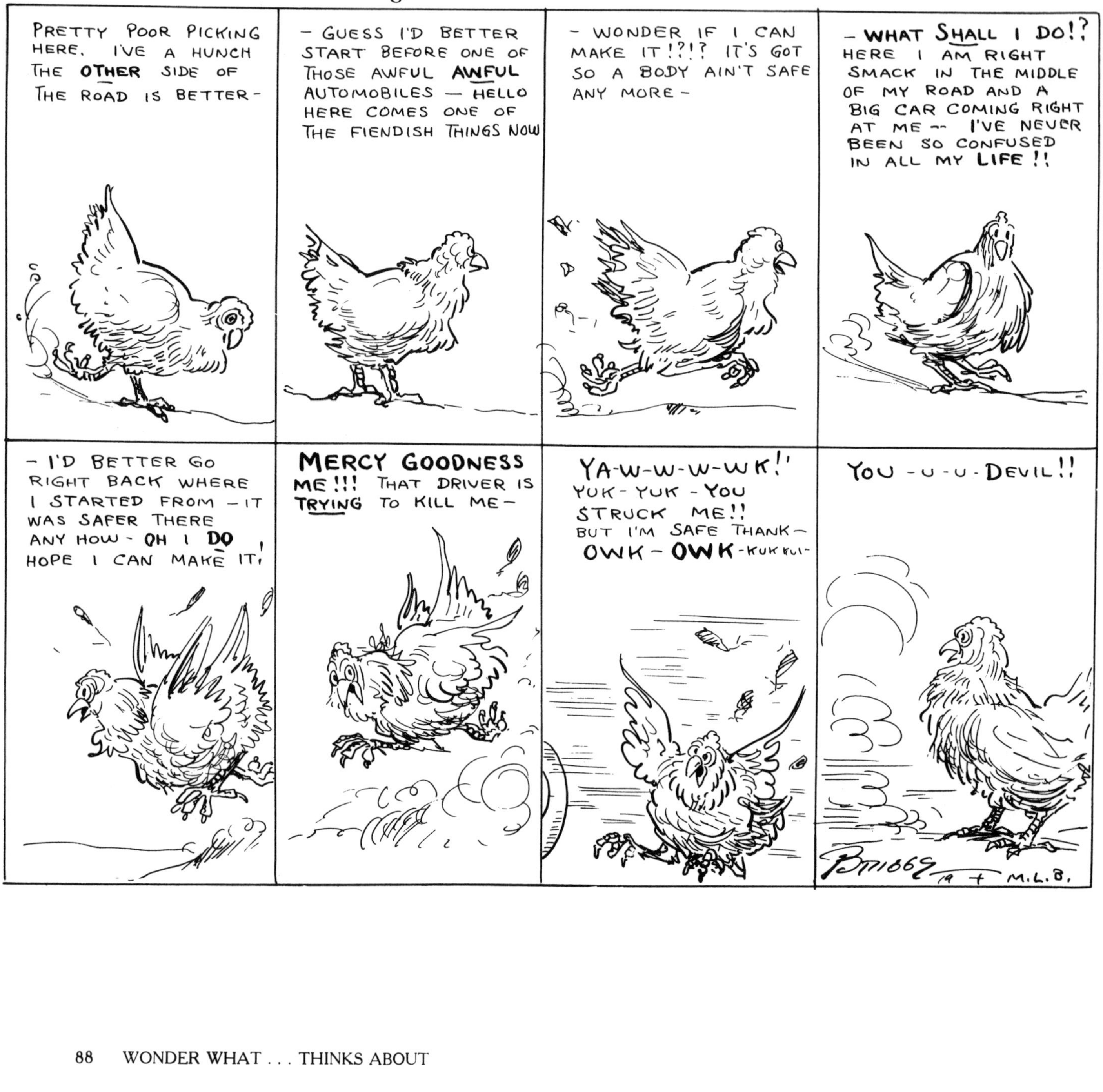

# *Movie of a Man Trying to Handle a Sunday Paper on a Windy Porch*

## *Movie of a Man Talking to His Year Old Child on the Phone*

## *Movie of a Man Watching His Daughter Don the Make-up*

# *Movie of a Man Wondering What to Buy the Wife for Christmas*

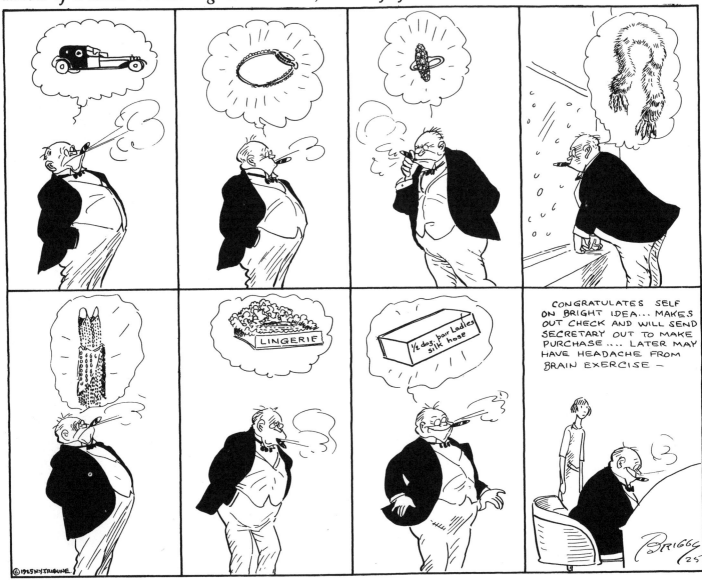

## Movie of a Man Toting a Watermelon

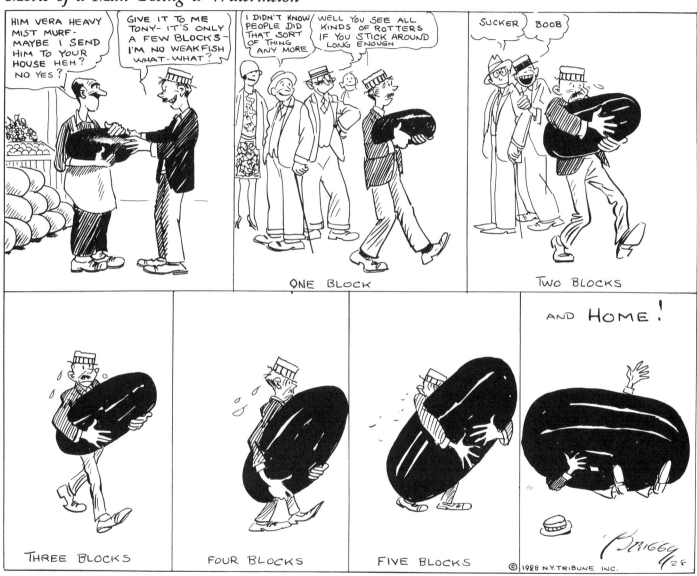

## Holding Hands Up

## Waiting for the Rest of the Family to Get Up

YOU AWAKE........ A GLANCE AT THE CLOCK SHOWS IT TO BE FIVE O'CLOCK

YOU SIT UP AND OBSERVE YOUR FOND PARENTS IN DEEP SLUMBER

YOU CALL FIRST TO MA

THEN YOU CALL TO PA

SINCE NEITHER OF THEM SHOW ANY VISIBLE INTEREST IN YOU, YOU SIT DOWN TO PONDER OVER THE SITUATION

YOU DECIDE TO PUT UP A SLIGHT SQUAWL JUST TO FEEL THEM OUT

STILL GETTING NO RESPONSE YOU DECIDE TO OPEN BOTH BARRELS AND GIVE THEM THE WHOLE WORKS

HAH! THAT STARTED 'EM

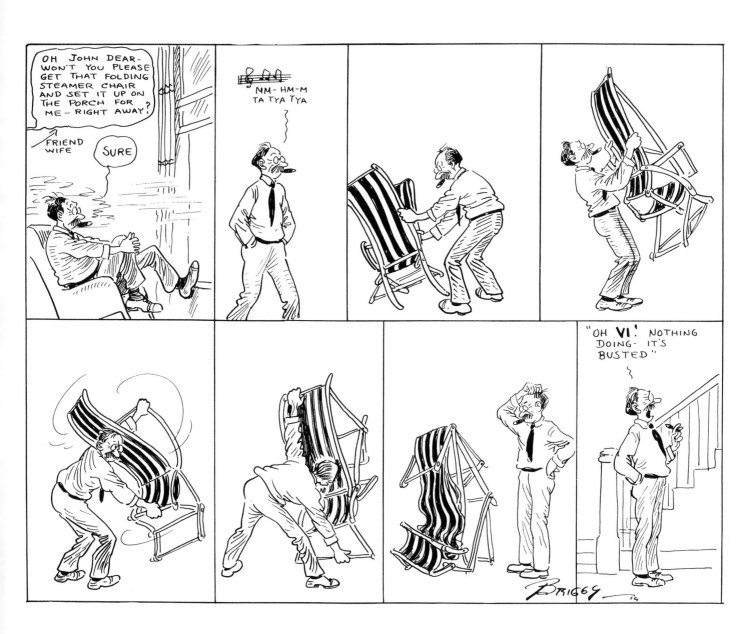

HANDY MAN AROUND THE HOUSE

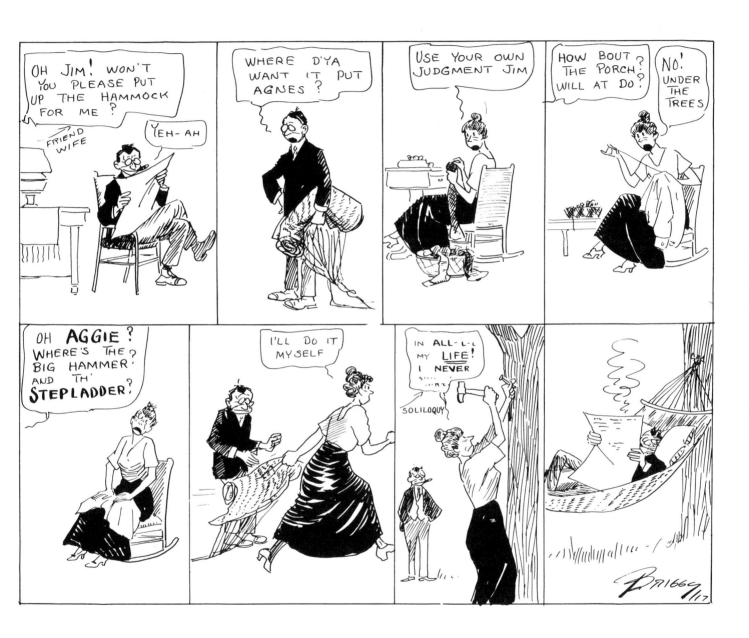

## Trying to Rattle Him

## At Home

SHEEZ MY YANNIE
I'M HER JOE
SHEEZ MY SWEE-TART
I'M HER BO-
SOON WEEL MARREE
NEVORE TO PAHRT
LITTLE ANNEE
ROON- EE
IS MY-Y-Y-
SWEE-E-E
-TART
BRIGGS '28

THE O-O-OLD OAK-EN BUCKIT!
THE I-I-IRON BOUND-D- BUCKIT
THAH MAW-W-W-S COVERED- BUCKIT-
THAT HAHNG-G-G IN THUH- WELL-L-
(IN THUH- WELL-L-L-L)
YATTA BABY!
GREAT STUFF
LET'S ALL DO IT AGAIN
SOME BASS EH?
©1925 N.Y. TRIBUNE INC.
BRIGGS '25

## The Lonesomest Soul in the World

## The Rich Man Goes Golfing

## *Why We Dub So Many Golf Shots—Hurrying*

## And Then He Took Up Golf

## *Captains of Industry*